THE
FOUR
INGREDIENT
COOKBOOK®

By Linda Coffee and Emily Cale

Coffee & Cale

P.O. Box 2121 • Kerrville, TX 78029 • 1-800-757-0838

www.fouringredientcookbook.com • email: areglen@ktc.com

For Wholesale Information: (830) 895-5528

ACKNOWLEDGMENTS

To our husbands, Mike and Bob, who had to listen to us, had to try everything, had to help with car pools; a special thanks to Bob for providing the computer equipment; to Stan Coffee who acted as consultant for the computer program; to our kids who only rolled their eyes slightly when we said we were going to "work on" a cookbook with recipes that even they could cook.

to our families

EMILY CALE

Born in San Antonio, Texas, Emily was raised in a military family who lived in Japan, Germany, Alaska, and all over the United States. Now living in Kerrville, Texas, she is married with two children and two stepchildren, one graduated from college, two in college and one in high school (and the college students have all received copies of **"The Four Ingredient Cookbook"**).

Emily has studied foreign gourmet cooking, and has participated in several gourmet cooking groups. Before moving to Kerrville, she worked at the United States Olympic Training Center in Colorado Springs. When she isn't busy promoting The Four Ingredient Cookbook©", she works at the Adult and Community Education Center (Club Ed) for the Kerrville Independent School District.

LINDA COFFEE

As a Home Economist, Linda worked in a foods and nutrition program as an Extension Agent for Texas A & M University. She has also been an interior designer and home designer, working with her husband's home building business.

The Coffees moved to Kerrville from Houston in 1977, in search of less traffic, a good environment to raise their two children, but the pace has been rather hectic! Their teenagers are active in football, track, volleyball and tennis.

Between her children's commitments, her husband's business and promoting "The Four Ingredient Cookbook©", Linda finds time to teach a Special Education class at Tivy High School.

SEASONINGS

The seasoning or lack of seasoning in a recipe is often a matter of preference, a necessity of diet or a daring experiment. We encourage you to enhance any of these simple recipes by adding seasoning of your choice; therefore, we have often used the expression "season to taste".

TABLE OF CONTENTS

APPETIZERS

COTTAGE CHEESE DIP

1.   1 Carton (24 oz.) Cottage Cheese
2.   1 Envelope Herb-Ox Dry Broth Mix
3.   1/3 Cup Milk

Blend all ingredients, chill and serve with chips or fresh vegetables.

DILL DIP

1.   1 Carton (12 oz.) Cottage Cheese
2.   2 1/2 Teaspoons Dill
3.   1/4 Teaspoon Seasoned Salt
4.   2 Tablespoons Lemon Juice

Combine all ingredients in blender. Blend at low speed. Refrigerate several hours for better flavor. Sprinkle with additional dill and serve with fresh vegetables.

CREAMY DILL DIP

1.   1 Cup Miracle Whip
2.   2 Tablespoons Onion (finely chopped)
3.   1 Tablespoon Milk
4.   1 Teaspoon Dill

Mix all ingredients and chill. Serve with fresh vegetables.

SPRING VEGETABLE DIP

1. 1 Envelope Dry Vegetable Soup Mix
2. 1 Pint Sour Cream

Combine soup mix and sour cream. Chill. Serve with chips or vegetables.

SOUR CREAM DIP

1. 1 Cup Sour Cream
2. 1/2 Tablespoon Prepared Mustard
3. 2 Tablespoons Chili Sauce
4. 1/4 Teaspoon Celery Seed

Combine all ingredients. Chill. Serve with celery sticks or cucumber slices.

AVOCADO AND LEEK DIP

1. 1 Large Ripe Avocado (mashed)
2. 1 Tablespoon Fresh Lemon Juice
3. 1/2 Package Dry Leek Soup Mix
4. 1 Cup Sour Cream

Mix mashed avocado with lemon juice. Combine with soup mix and sour cream. Serve with corn chips or tortilla chips.

CREAM CHEESE DIP

1.   1 Package (8 oz.) Cream Cheese
2.   1 1/2 Tablespoons Lemon Juice
3.   1 1/2 Teaspoons Onion (grated)
4.   2 Cups Sour Cream

Let cream cheese soften at room temperature. Cream until smooth. Add lemon juice and onion, blend well. Gradually blend in sour cream. Chill. Serve with potato chips, crackers or fresh vegetables.

FRESH FRUIT DIP

1.   Assorted Fresh Fruits (cut in bite-size pieces)
2.   1 Cup Sour Cream
3.   1 Tablespoon Brown Sugar

Mix sour cream and brown sugar. Add granulated sugar for desired sweetness. Serve with fruits.

SWEET FRUIT DIP

1.   1 Jar (7 oz.) Marshmallow Cream
2.   1 Package (8 oz.) Cream Cheese
3.   1 Carton (8 oz.) Sour Cream
4.   1 Can (14 oz.) Sweetened Condensed Milk

Combine all ingredients in container of an electric blender and blend until smooth. Chill at least 1 hour. Serve with assorted fruits.

TOMATO-SOUR CREAM DIP

1.   1 Can (8 oz.) Tomato Sauce
2.   1 Cup Sour Cream
3.   2 Teaspoons Grated Onion
4.   1 Teaspoon Horseradish

Combine all ingredients. Chill. Serve with chips or fresh vegetables.

HOT SEAFOOD DIP

1.   3 (8 oz. each) Packages Cream Cheese
2.   6 Tablespoons Milk
3.   2 Tablespoons Worcestershire Sauce
4.   1 Can (6 1/2 oz.) Crab Meat

Soften cream cheese to room temperature. Mix all ingredients and place into a small ovenproof casserole. Bake 15 minutes at 350 degrees. Serve with chips or crackers.

CHILI DIP

1.   1 Can (15 oz.) Chili Without Beans
2.   1 Package (8 oz.) Cream Cheese
3.   1/2 Cup Green Chili Sauce or Jalapeno Salsa
4.   1 Can (2 1/2 oz.) Sliced Black Olives (drained)

Combine chili and cream cheese in pan. Cook over low heat until cheese melts, stirring occasionally. Stir in sauce and olives. Serve with tortilla chips.

CHILI CON QUESO-I

1.   2 Jalapeno Peppers, reserve 1 tablespoon liquid
2.   1 Jar (16 oz.) Processed Cheese Spread
3.   1 Jar (4 oz.) Pimentos (drained and chopped)

Seed jalapeno peppers and chop. Combine peppers, cheese spread and pimentos in saucepan. Heat on stove, stirring constantly, until cheese melts. Stir in reserved liquid. Serve with tortilla chips.

CHILI CON QUESO-II

1.   1 Pound Velveeta Cheese (melted)
2.   1 Can (15 oz.) Chili With Beans
3.   1 Can (4 oz.) Green Chiles (chopped)
4.   1 Medium Onion (finely chopped)

Mix all ingredients and bake in deep container for 35 minutes at 350 degrees. Serve with chips.

ZIPPY CHEESE DIP

1.   1 Pound Ground Beef
2.   1 Pound Velveeta Cheese (cubed)
3.   1 Jar (8 oz.) Picante Sauce

Brown ground beef and drain well. Melt cheese and add picante sauce. Combine meat and cheese mixture. Serve hot with tortilla chips.

CHEESE SPREAD DIP

1.   1 Jar (8 oz.) Processed Cheese Spread
2.   2 Tablespoons Dry White Wine
3.   2 Teaspoons Prepared Mustard
4.   1/2 Teaspoon Worcestershire Sauce

Mix all ingredients. Chill. Serve with pretzels.

HOT CHEESE DIP

1.   1 Pound Velveeta Cheese (cubed)
2.   2 Cups Mayonnaise
3.   1 Small Onion (chopped)
4.   3 Jalapeno Peppers (seeded and chopped)

Place cheese in saucepan and melt over low heat. Add
other ingredients and mix well. Serve with crackers or
fresh vegetables.

SAN ANTONE BEAN DIP

1.   1 Can (10 1/4 oz.) Condensed Black Bean Soup
2.   1 Can (8 oz.) Tomato Sauce
3.   1 Cup Sour Cream
4.   1/2 Teaspoon Chili Powder

Heat all ingredients in saucepan. Stir mixture occasionally.
Serve with tortilla chips.

MEXICAN DIP

1.   1 Pound Ground Beef
2.   1/2 Pound Mexican Velveeta Cheese (cubed)
3.   2/3 Cup Miracle Whip
4.   1/4 Cup Onion (chopped)

Season to taste and brown meat; drain. Add remaining ingredients and mix well. Spoon mixture into a 9-inch pie plate. Bake 10 minutes at 350 degrees. Stir and continue to bake 5 minutes longer. Serve with corn chips.

REAL GOOD DIP

1.   1 Pound Lean Hamburger
2.   1 Pound Jimmy Dean Sausage (hot)
3.   1 Pound Mexican Velveeta Cheese (cubed)
4.   1 Can Golden Mushroom Soup

Brown hamburger and sausage. Drain. Add cheese and soup and heat over low temperature until cheese is melted and thoroughly blended. Serve with tortilla chips.

SERVING IDEA - Form a "bowl" for serving dip by scooping out the center of a round, unsliced loaf of bread. Make croutons or bread crumbs from the bread when it has served its' purpose as a "bowl".

LOBSTER DIP

1.   2 Tablespoons Margarine
2.   2 Cups Sharp American Cheese (shredded)
3.   1/3 Cup Dry White Wine
4.   1 Can (5 oz.) Lobster (drained)

Melt margarine and gradually stir in cheese. Break lobster into pieces. Stir in wine and lobster. Heat thoroughly and serve with chips or crackers.

CHILI HAM SPREAD

1.   1 Can (4 1/4 oz.) Deviled Ham
2.   1 Tablespoon Mayonnaise
3.   1 Teaspoon Grated Onion
4.   1 Jalapeno Pepper (finely chopped)

Mix all ingredients. Spread on crackers.

COTTAGE CHEESE-CUCUMBER SPREAD

1.   1 Cup Cucumber (finely chopped)
2.   1 Cup Small Curd Cottage Cheese
3.   Dash Pepper
4.   Minced Chives

Mix cucumber, cottage cheese and pepper. Spread on crackers and garnish with minced chives.

HOT ARTICHOKE CANAPES

1.   1 Cup Mayonnaise
2.   1 Cup Freshly Grated Parmesan Cheese
3.   1 Can (4 oz.) Green Chiles (drained and chopped)
4.   1 Cup Of Canned Water Packed Artichoke Hearts
      (chopped/drained)

Mix mayonnaise, parmesan cheese, green chilies and artichoke hearts. Put 1 teaspoon of the mixture on bite-size
toast rounds. Broil until lightly brown.

RICOTTA CRACKERS

1.   Crackers (wheat, rye or any firm cracker)
2.   1 Cup Ricotta Cheese
3.   1/2 Cup Chutney
4.   1/4 Cup Nuts (chopped)

Blend cheese and chutney and spread each cracker with
mixture. Sprinkle with 1/4 teaspoon chopped nuts.

HIDDEN VALLEY RANCH CHEESE PUFFS

1.   2 Cups Shredded Sharp Cheddar Cheese
2.   3/4 Cup Mayonnaise
3.   1 Tablespoon Hidden Valley Ranch Milk Mix
4.   10 (1-inch) Slices French Bread

Mix first three ingredients. Spread on bread slices. Broil
until golden brown (about 3 minutes).

NUTTY CREAM CHEESE SPREAD

1.   2 Packages (8 oz. each) Cream Cheese
2.   1/2 Cup Sour Cream
3.   1 Package (4 oz.) Ranch Style Salad Dressing
4.   1 Package (2 oz.) Pecan Chips

Combine first 3 ingredients, stirring until blended. Chill 10 minutes. Shape mixture into a log. Lightly coat top and sides with pecans. Serve with crackers.

PINEAPPLE BALL

1 Package (8 oz.) Cream Cheese
1 Can (3 1/2 oz.) Crushed Pineapple (drained_
2 Tablespoons Green Pepper (chopped)
1 Teaspoon Lawry's Seasoned Salt

Mix cream cheese, pineapple, green pepper and Lawry's Seasoned Salt. Shape into a ball and serve with crackers.

SHRIMP SPREAD

1.   2 Cans (4 1/2 oz. each) Shrimp (drained)
2.   2 Cups Mayonnaise
3.   6 Green Onions (chopped fine)

Crumble shrimp. Mix above ingredients and refrigerate for at least one hour. Serve with crackers.

HOT CELERY APPETIZER

1.   Crackers Or Rye Bread
2.   3 Ounces Cream Cheese
3.   1/4 Cup Concentrated Celery Soup
4.   1 Cup Salami (ground)

Combine cream cheese, soup and ground salami. Spread mixture on crackers or bread. Heat under broiler until brown.

DEVILED HAM APPETIZER

1.   Crackers
2.   1 Can (4 1/4 oz.) Deviled Ham
3.   1/2 Teaspoon Lemon Juice
4.   1/2 Teaspoon Worcestershire Sauce

Mix deviled ham, lemon juice and Worcestershire sauce. Spread on crackers.

PIZZA CRACKERS

1.   4 Dozen Melba Or Cracker Rounds
2.   3/4 Cup Ketchup
3.   2 Ounces Thinly Sliced Pepperoni
4.   1 Cup Shredded Mozzarella Cheese

Spread rounds with ketchup and top with pepperoni slices. Sprinkle with cheese and bake on cookie sheet 3 to 5 minutes at 400 degrees.

EASY CRAB SPREAD

1.   1 Package (8 oz.) Cream Cheese
2.   1 Bottle (12 oz.) Cocktail Sauce
3.   1 Can (6 oz.) Crab Meat (drained)

Spread cream cheese on dinner plate and pour bottle of cocktail sauce over cream cheese. Crumble crab meat on top of the cocktail sauce. Serve with crackers.

GARLIC LOAF

1.   1 Can Refrigerator Biscuits (separated)
2.   1/2 Cup Margarine (melted)
3.   1 Teaspoon Garlic Powder
4.   1 Tablespoon Parsley

Cut each biscuit in half. Mix garlic, parsley and margarine. Dip biscuits in mixture and place in 9-inch pie plate. Bake 15 minutes at 400 degrees.

CRISPY CHEESE BREAD

1.   2/3 Cups Crushed Rice Chex Cereal
2.   3 Tablespoons Parmesan Cheese
3.   2 Tablespoons Margarine (melted)
4.   1 Can Refrigerated Biscuits (separated)

Combine cereal, cheese, margarine. Halve biscuits. Coat with crumb mixture. Place biscuits on cut edge in 9-inch pie plate and bake 15 minutes at 400 degrees.

SAUSAGE CHEESE TURNOVERS

1.   10 (1 oz.) Link Sausages (cooked until brown)
2.   2 Ounces Sharp Cheddar Cheese Strips
3.   1 Can (11 oz.) Refrigerated Biscuits
4.   2 Tablespoons Cornmeal

Roll each biscuit into a 4-inch diameter circle; sprinkle with cornmeal. Center cheese strips and sausages on biscuits. Fold over and seal edges with fork dipped in flour. Bake 10 minutes 400 degrees.

BACON ROLL-UPS

1.   1/2 Cup Sour Cream
2.   1/2 Teaspoon Onion Salt
3.   1/2 Pound Bacon (cooked and crumbled)
4.   1 Package (8 oz.) Crescent Rolls (separated)

Mix the top 3 ingredients; spread on rolls and roll up. Place on baking sheet. Bake 12-15 minutes at 375 degrees.

MORNING COFFEE APPETIZER

1.   1 Package Pre-cooked Pork Link Sausage
2.   1 Package Refrigerator Butterflake Rolls

Cut each sausage in thirds. Peel two thin sections off a Butterflake roll; wrap around a small piece of sausage. Bake on ungreased cookie sheet 7-8 minutes at 450 degrees.

SAUSAGE CHEESE BALLS

1.   1 Pound Hot Pork Sausage
2.   1 Pound Sharp Cheddar Cheese (grated)
3.   3 Cups Biscuit Mix
4.   1/4 to 1/2 Cup Water

Mix all ingredients and form into bite-size balls. Bake 10 to 15 minutes at 375 degrees.

OLIVE CHEESE BALLS

1.   2 Cups Shredded Sharp Cheddar Cheese
2.   1 1/4 Cups All-Purpose Flour
3.   1/2 Cup Margarine (melted)
4.   36 Small Pimiento Stuffed Olives (drained)

Mix cheese and flour; mix in margarine. From this dough mixture, mold 1 teaspoonful around each olive. Shape into a ball. Place on ungreased cookie sheet and refrigerate at least 1 hour. Bake 15 to 20 minutes at 400 degrees.

PARTY BISCUITS

1.   1 Cup Self-rising Flour
2.   1 Cup Whipping Cream (not whipped)
3.   3 Tablespoons Sugar

Mix ingredients and pour into greased mini-muffin cups. Bake 10 minutes at 400 degrees.

CHEESE ROUNDS

1.   1 Cup Cheddar Cheese (grated)
2.   1/2 Cup Margarine
3.   1 1/4 Cup Flour
4.   Dash Cayenne Pepper

Mix ingredients and form long rolls 1-inch in diameter.
When ready to bake, slice into 1/4-inch rounds and bake 5
minutes at 400 degrees.

CHEESE STICKS

1.   1 Loaf Regular Slice Bread (crust removed)
2.   1/2 Cup Margarine (melted)
3.   1 Cup Parmesan Cheese
4.   1 Teaspoon Paprika

Slice bread into thin sticks. Roll in melted margarine, then
in Parmesan and paprika. Place on cookie sheet. Bake 20
minutes at 325 degrees.

BEER BISCUITS

1.   3 Cups Biscuit Mix
2.   1/4 Teaspoon Salt
3.   1 Teaspoon Sugar
4.   1 1/2 Cups Beer

Mix all ingredients and spoon into 12 greased muffin cups.
Bake 15 minutes at 425 degrees.

PARTY RYE BREAD

1. 1 Package Party Rye Bread
2. 1 Cup Mayonnaise
3. 3/4 Cup Parmesan Cheese
4. 1 Onion (grated)

Mix mayonnaise, cheese and onion. Spread on bread and broil 2-3 minutes.

WATER CHESTNUTS

1. 2 Cans (8 oz. each) Whole Water Chestnuts
2. 6 to 8 Slices Bacon (cut into quarters)

Wrap each water chestnut with quartered strip of bacon. Secure with toothpick. Broil until bacon is cooked.

WATER CHESTNUT APPETIZERS

1. 1 (8 oz.) Water Chestnuts
2. 6 Thin Slices Bacon (halved)
3. 6 Chicken Livers (halved)
4. Hot English Mustard

Divide water chestnuts into 12 portions. Wrap each chestnut with liver, then a piece of bacon. Secure with toothpick and broil until bacon is crisp. Serve with hot English mustard as a dip.

BACON SURPRISE

1.   1 Pound Bacon
2.   1/2 Cup Brown Sugar
3.   1 Jar (7 3/4 oz.) Pickled Onions (drained)
4.   Dash of Dry Mustard (optional))

Cut bacon into fourths. Wrap a piece of bacon around a pickled onion. Secure with toothpick and roll in brown sugar. Place on broiler pan and broil until bacon is crisp.

FRIED MOZZARELLA

1.   8 Ounces Mozzarella (cut in 1/2-inch cubes)
2.   2 Eggs (slightly beaten)
3.   1 Cup Fine Cracker Crumbs
4.   2 Tablespoons Olive Oil

Dip the cheese cubes into the egg and then into the cracker crumbs. Heat the oil in a skillet and fry the breaded cheese until crisp and brown. Stick each cube with a toothpick.

VIENNA COCKTAIL SAUSAGES

1.   2/3 Cup Prepared Mustard
2.   1 Cup Currant Jelly
3.   4 Cans (4 oz. each) Vienna Sausages (halved)
4.   Pinch of Salt (optional)

Mix mustard and jelly. Add sausages; heat thoroughly; serve hot.

JALAPENO PIE

1.   1/4 to 1/2 Cup Sliced Jalapenos
2.   3 Eggs (beaten)
3.   2 Cups Grated Cheddar Cheese
4.   Salt And Pepper To Taste

Place peppers in greased 9-inch pie plate...you can adjust amount of peppers to your taste. Sprinkle cheese over peppers. Pour seasoned eggs over cheese. Bake 20 minutes at 400 degrees. Cut into small slices and serve.

DEVILED EGGS

1.   6 Hard Cooked Eggs
2.   1 1/2 Tablespoons Sweet Pickle Relish
3.   3 Tablespoons Mayonnaise
4.   Paprika

Peel eggs and cut in half lengthwise. Take yolks out and mash with fork. Add relish and mayonnaise to yolks. Place the yolk mixture back into the egg white halves. Sprinkle with paprika.

PREPARATION IDEA - When grating cheese, brush the grater with oil or spray with no stick cooking spray for easy clean up.

STUFFED MUSHROOMS

1.   1 Pound Mushrooms (half dollar size)
2.   1 Cup Bread Crumbs
3.   2 Tablespoons Margarine
4.   2 Slices Ham Lunch Meat (chopped)

Remove stems and inside of mushrooms. Chop stems and mix with remaining ingredients. Stuff mushrooms and place in buttered casserole dish. Bake 15 minutes at 350 degrees.

DRIED BEEF BALLS

1.   3 Ounces Cream Cheese
2.   1/2 Teaspoon Minced Onion
3.   3 Ounces Dried Beef
4.   1/4 Teaspoon Garlic Powder (optional)

Chop beef and add onion and cream cheese. Form into small balls and refrigerate. Serve with toothpicks.

SERVING IDEA - Appetizers served individually on toothpicks can be stuck into a grapefruit for an easy, attractive way to serve.

VEGETABLES

ASPARAGUS ROLL UP

1.   4 Slices Ham
2.   4 Slices Swiss Cheese
3.   2 Cans (10 1/2 oz. each) Asparagus Spears
4.   1 Cup Sour Cream

Place a slice of cheese on top of each ham slice. Put 3 asparagus spears on each ham/cheese slice. Roll up, secure with toothpick. Place in casserole, seam side down and spoon sour cream over each roll. Bake 15 minutes at 350 degrees. Serves 4.

BAKED BEANS

1.   2 Tablespoons Brown Sugar
2.   1 Tablespoon Mustard
3.   1 Cup Ketchup
4.   2 Cans (15 oz. each) Pork And Beans

Combine all ingredients. Bake 1 hour at 350 degrees. Serves 6-8.

SPICY GREEN BEANS

1   2 Cans (16 oz. each) Green Beans (drained)
2.   4 Slices Bacon (chopped)
3.   1 Medium Onion (chopped)
4.   1/4 Cup Vinegar

Sauté bacon and onion in skillet. Drain. Add green beans and vinegar and heat thoroughly.

BUSH'S BROCCOLI SALAD

1.   3 Cups Broccoli (cut into bite-size pieces)
2.   1 Red Onion (chopped)
3.   1 Cup Cheddar Cheese (grated)
4.   6 Slices Bacon (cooked and crumbled)

Combine all ingredients. Best when used with the following dressing. Serves 6-8.

BROCCOLI DRESSING

1.   1 Cup Mayonnaise
2.   1/4 Cup Sugar
3.   2 Tablespoons Vinegar
4.   Broccoli Salad

Mix well and pour over broccoli salad (see above salad).

MARINATED BRUSSELS SPROUTS

1   3 Packages (10.oz. each) Brussels Sprouts (cooked)
2.   1/2 Cup Salad Oil
3.   1/4 Cup White Wine Vinegar
4.   1 Package Italian Salad Dressing Mix

Combine oil, vinegar and packaged Italian salad dressing mix and pour over brussel sprouts. Marinate overnight. Serve cold. Serves 6-8.

HOT CABBAGE

1.   3 Cups Cabbage (finely chopped)
2   1/2 Teaspoon Salt
3.   2 Tablespoons Vegetable Oil
4.   2 Tablespoons Italian Salad Dressing

Sprinkle cabbage with salt and set aside for 30 minutes. Heat oil in skillet until very hot. Add the cabbage and stir fry about 2 minutes. Remove and add Italian dressing. Serves 4.

PEACHY CARROTS

1.   1 Pound Package Carrots (sliced and cooked)
2.   1/3 Cup Peach Preserves
3.   1 Tablespoon Margarine (melted)

Combine carrots with margarine and peach preserves. Cook over low heat until carrots are heated thoroughly. Serves 6.

CARROT CASSEROLE

1.   1 Pound Package Carrots (sliced, cooked until tender)
2.   1/2 Cup Celery (chopped)
3.   1/3 Cup Onion (chopped)
4.   1/3 Cup Green Pepper (chopped)

Sauté chopped celery, onion and green pepper. Mash cooked carrots and mix with sautéed vegetables. Put in buttered baking dish. Bake 30 minutes at 350. Serves 6.

HONEY CARROTS

1. 1 Pound Package Carrots (peeled and sliced)
2. 1/4 Cup Honey
3. 1/4 Cup Margarine (melted)
4. 1/4 Cup Brown Sugar (firmly packed)

Cook carrots in small amount of boiling water for 5 to 10 minutes or until crisp-tender. Drain, reserve 1/4 cup of the carrot liquid. Combine reserved liquid, honey, margarine, brown sugar. Stir well and pour over carrots. Cook over low heat until heated thoroughly. Serves 6.

CREAM CHEESE CORN

1. 2 Cans (16 oz. each) Whole Corn (drained)
2. 1 Package (8 oz.) Cream Cheese
3. 1 Can (4 oz.) Green Chiles (chopped)
4. 1 Tablespoon Margarine

Combine ingredients in saucepan. Simmer over low heat until cheese melts. Mix well. Serves 4-6.

CORN PUDDING

1. 2 Cans (16 oz. each) Creamed Corn
2. 1 Package (6 oz.) Corn Muffin Mix
3. 2 Eggs (beaten)
4. 1/2 Cup Margarine (melted)

Mix all ingredients and pour into a greased 2 quart casserole dish. Bake 45 minutes at 350 degrees. Serves 6.

CORN CASSEROLE

1.   2 Cans (16 oz. each) Cream Corn
2.   1/2 Cup Milk
3.   1 Cup Bread Crumbs
4.   1/2 Cup Green Pepper (chopped)

Mix all ingredients and pour into casserole. Bake 30 minutes at 350 degrees. Serves 4-6.

OKRA GUMBO

1.   2 Slices Bacon (chopped)
2.   1/2 Cup Onion (chopped)
3.   1 Package (10 oz.) Frozen Okra (sliced)
4.   1 Can (14 1/2 oz.) Stewed Tomatoes (chopped)

Sauté bacon, add onion and brown. Add frozen okra and stewed tomatoes. Cook over low heat until okra is tender. Season to taste. Serves 4-6.

ONION CUSTARD

1.   4-6 Medium Mild Onions (thinly sliced)
2.   3 Tablespoons Unsalted Butter
3.   1 Cup Milk
4.   3 Eggs

Sauté onions in butter in covered skillet for 30 minutes. Cool. In bowl beat together milk and eggs. Stir in onions and transfer to greased baking dish. Bake 40-50 minutes at 325 degrees or until light golden. Serves 6-8.

BAKED ONION RINGS

1.   2 Egg Whites
2.   1 Large Sweet Yellow Onion (cut into rings)
3.   1/3 Cup Dry Bread Crumbs
4.   Salt And Pepper To Taste

Mix egg whites, salt and pepper. Dip onion rings into egg mixture and then coat with breadcrumbs. Place in single layer on greased baking sheet. Bake 10 minutes at 450 degrees. Serves 4.

SOUFFLE POTATO

1.   2 2/3 Cups Mashed Potato Mix
2.   1 Egg (beaten)
3.   1 Can (2.8 oz) French Fried Onion Rings
4.   1/2 Cup Shredded Cheddar Cheese

Prepare mashed potato mix according to package directions. Add egg, onions and stir until blended. Spoon mixture into a lightly greased 1 quart dish. Sprinkle with cheese. Bake uncovered 5 minutes at 350 degrees. Serves 6.

BAKED POTATO TOPPING

1.   1 Cup Sharp Processed Cheese (grated)
2.   1/2 Cup Sour Cream
3.   1/4 Cup Soft Margarine
4.   4 Tablespoons Green Onion (chopped)

Mix all ingredients and serve on baked potato. Serves 4-6.

TWICE BAKED POTATOES

1.   4 Baked Potatoes
2.   4 Tablespoons Margarine
3.   1/2 Cup Milk
4.   1 Cup Cheddar Cheese (grated)

Bake potatoes. Cut cooked potatoes in half. Scoop out meat of the potato and whip with margarine and milk. Mound back into the potato halves. Sprinkle with grated cheese. Bake 30 minutes at 350 degrees. Serves 4-8.

SHEEPHERDER POTATOES

1.   8 Bacon Slices (minced)
2.   2 Onions (chopped)
3.   4 Potatoes (peeled, sliced 1/2-inch thick)
4.   Salt And Pepper

Fry bacon until not quite crisp. Add onion and sauté until limp. Pour off all but 2 tablespoons of drippings. Center potatoes on tin foil placed in large casserole dish. Pour bacon mixture over potatoes and season with salt and pepper. Seal foil with small space between potatoes and foil. Bake 1 1/2 hours at 300 degrees. Serves 4-6.

PREPARATION IDEA - Freeze stale bread and then grate the frozen bread to use as vegetable or casserole toppers as needed.

RICE-GREEN CHILI CASSEROLE

1.　　1 Can (4 oz.) Chopped Green Chiles (drained)
2.　　2 Cups Sour Cream
3.　　3 Cups Cooked White Rice
4.　　8 Ounces Monterrey Jack Cheese (grated)

Combine chilies and sour cream. Place 1 cup cooked rice in bottom of 1 1/2 quart casserole. Spoon a third of sour cream mixture over rice and top with one third of the cheese. Do this two more times. Cover and bake 20 minutes at 350 degrees. Uncover and bake 10 minutes longer. Serves 6.

MEXICAN RICE

1.　　1 Cup Uncooked Minute Rice
2.　　1 Green Pepper (chopped)
3.　　1/2 Medium Onion (chopped)
4.　　1 Can (28 oz.) Diced Tomatoes

Fry 3 tablespoons of the uncooked rice until brown. Add onions and green pepper and sauté. Add rest of uncooked rice and can of tomatoes (add a little water if needed). Cover and simmer 1/2 hour. Serves 4-6.

SERVING IDEA - Many cooked vegetables taste wonderful just tossed with margarine. Add variety to the margarine with spices. For example, add 1 teaspoon celery seed or 2 tablespoons grated Parmesan cheese or 1/4 teaspoon garlic powder to 1/4 cup margarine.

SNOW PEAS AND MUSHROOMS

1.   1 Cup Sliced Mushrooms
2.   2 Tablespoons Margarine
3.   1/2 Pound Small Snow Peas
4.   1 Tablespoon Soy Sauce

Sauté mushrooms in margarine. Stir in snow peas and soy sauce. Cook until crisp-tender. Toss and serve. Serves 4.

SQUASH CASSEROLE

1.   6 Medium Yellow Squash (sliced)
2.   1 Small Onion (chopped)
3.   1 Cup Velveeta Cheese (cut in 1/2-inch cubes)
4.   1 Can (4 oz.) Chopped Green Chiles

Boil squash and onion until tender. Drain well and mix with cheese and chilies. Pour into buttered baking dish. Bake 15 minutes at 375 degrees. Serves 6-8.

"HOT" ZUCCHINI SQUASH

1.   5-6 Medium Zucchini (sliced in round)
2.   1 Cup Monterrey Jack Jalapeno Cheese (grated)
3.   1/2 Cup Bread Crumbs
4.   1 Can (14 1/2 oz.) Stewed Tomatoes (chopped)

Boil zucchini for 8 minutes until crisp-tender. Place 1/2 of zucchini in greased casserole and sprinkle with cheese and crumbs. Top with remainder of zucchini. Cover with tomatoes. Bake 30 minutes at 350 degrees. Serves 6-8.

ZUCCHINI SQUASH FRITTERS

1. 2 Medium Zucchini (grated)
2. 1 Carrot (grated)
3. 1 Egg (beaten)
4. 1/2 Cup Flour

Mix all ingredients. Drop by tablespoon into 1/2-inch oil in skillet. Fry until golden brown. Drain on paper towel and serve. Serves 4-6.

SPINACH CASSEROLE I

1 Carton (16 oz.) Cottage Cheese
8 Ounces Sharp Cheddar Cheese (grated)
1 Package (10 oz.)
3 Eggs (beaten)

Combine all ingredients and mix well. Spoon into buttered casserole. Bake 45 minutes at 350 degrees. Serves 6.

SPINACH CASSEROLE II

3 Boxes (10 oz. Each) Frozen Chopped Spinach
1 Cup Sour Cream
1 Envelope Dry Onion Soup Mix

Thaw spinach, press out water. Mix all ingredients. Bake 20-25 minutes at 325 degrees. Serves 8-10.

SWEET POTATO AND APPLE BAKE

1.   6 Large Sweet Potatoes (peeled, sliced, boiled)
2.   6 Tart Apples (peeled and sliced)
3.   1/2 Cup Margarine
4.   1/2 Cup Brown Sugar

Grease casserole with part of margarine. Layer potatoes, dot with margarine and sprinkle with brown sugar, layer with apple slices. Repeat, ending with potatoes, margarine and brown sugar. Bake 30-45 minutes at 350 degrees, or until potatoes are tender and browned. Serves 8-10.

TOMATO STACK

1.   1 Package (10 oz.) Frozen Chopped Broccoli
2.   1 Cup Grated Monterrey Jack Cheese
3.   1/4 Cup Onion (finely chopped)
4.   3 Large Tomatoes (halved)

Cook broccoli as directed. Drain and mix with cheese, reserve 2 tablespoons of cheese for top. Add onion. Place tomato halves in greased baking dish. Place broccoli mixture on each tomato half and top with reserved cheese. Broil 10-12 minutes at 350 degrees. Serves 6.

COLD VEGETABLE DISH

1.   1 Basket Cherry Tomatoes
2.   1 Bunch Broccoli (fresh and cut up)
3.   1 Head Cauliflower (fresh and cut up)
4.   1 Bottle (8 oz.) Italian Salad Dressing

Mix above ingredients the day before you are ready to serve. Serve cold. Serves 8-10.

MAIN
DISHES

BEEF-RICE CASSEROLE Bake 350 Degrees 1 Hour

1.   1 Pound Ground Round Or Lean Chuck
2.   2 Cans Cream Of Onion Soup
3.   1 Package Dry Onion Soup Mix
4.   1 Cup Rice (uncooked)

Mix all ingredients. Put in baking dish and bake covered.
Serves 4-6.

POORMAN STEAK   Bake 325 Degrees   1 Hour

1   3 Pounds Ground Beef
2.   1 Cup Cracker Crumbs
3.   1 Cup Water
4.   1 Can Cream Of Mushroom Soup

Combine ground beef, cracker crumbs, water and season to
taste. Form into serving size patties and brown in skillet.
Remove browned beef and put in oven roaster. Spread soup
on top and bake covered. Serves 8-10.

INDIAN CORN   Stove Top

1.   1 Pound Lean Hamburger
2.   1 Can (16 oz.) Whole Corn (drained)
3.   1/2 Onion (chopped)
4.   1 Jar (12 oz.) Taco Sauce

Brown hamburger and onion; add corn and taco sauce.
Simmer mixture for 5 minutes. Serve with tortilla chips.
Serves 4-6.

BBQ CUPS   **Bake 400 Degrees   12 Minutes**

1.   1 Pound Lean Ground Beef
2.   1/2 Cup Barbeque Sauce
3.   1 Can Refrigerator Biscuits
4.   3/4 Cup Grated Cheddar Cheese

Brown meat, drain. Add barbeque sauce and set aside.
Place biscuits in ungreased muffin cups, pressing dough up
sides to edge of cup. Spoon meat mixture into cups.
Sprinkle with cheese. Bake. Serves 4-5.

HAMBURGER IN OVEN **Bake 350 Degrees   30 Minutes**

1.   2 Pounds Extra Lean Ground Beef
2.   2 Medium Onions (sliced thin)
3.   1 Package (32 oz.) Frozen French Fries
4.   Salt and Pepper

Divide meat into 6-8 equal parts and make into patties.
Season to taste. Place on foil in large baking pan and arrange
onion slices on top of each patty. Place fries around them.
Wrap foil tightly and bake. Serves 6-8.

TATER TOT CASSEROLE   Bake 350 Degrees   1 Hour

1.   2 Pounds Extra Lean Ground Beef
2.   1 Can Cream Of Mushroom Soup
3.   1 Cup Grated Cheddar Cheese
4.   1 Package (2 lbs.) Frozen Tater Tots

Pat ground beef in bottom of greased 13x9x2 pan. Spread soup over meat and cover with grated cheese. Top with tater tots. Bake covered 45 minutes and uncovered 15 minutes. Serves 8-10.

SALISBURY STEAK   Stove Top

1.   1 Pound Lean Ground Beef
2.   1 Egg
3.   1 Medium Onion (chopped)
4.   1 Beef Bouillon Cube (dissolved in 1/2 cup water)

Mix beef, egg and onion. Shape into patties and brown over high heat, drain off any fat. Pour in bouillon and simmer uncovered until desired doneness. Serves 4.

BEEF PATTIES   Stove Top

1.   1 Pound Ground Beef Chuck
2.   1 Cup Mashed Potatoes
3.   2 Tablespoons Onion (minced)
4.   2 Tablespoons Margarine

Mix beef, potatoes, onion and form into patties. Brown slowly in margarine until desired doneness. Serves 4-6.

"FAST" FOOD MEXICAN   Bake 350 Degrees   30 Minutes

1. 1 Dozen Tamales (wrappers removed)
2. 1 Can (15 oz.) Chili
3. 1 Cup Onions (chopped)
4. 1 1/2 Cup Grated Cheddar Cheese

Place tamales in greased casserole, top with chili and sprinkle with cheese and onions. Bake. Serves 4.

QUICK ENCHILADAS   Bake 350 Degrees   45 Minutes

1. 2 Cans (15 oz. each) Hominy (drained)
2. 1 Cup Onion (chopped)
3. 2 Cups Grated Cheddar Cheese
4. 1 Can (15 oz.) Chili or Enchilada Sauce

Place hominy and onions in casserole. Top with 1/2 of cheese. Spread chili over top and then remainder of the cheese. Bake. Serves 4-6.

SUNDAY POT ROAST   Bake 350 Degrees   4 Hours

1. 4-6 Pound Chuck Roast
2. 1 Package Dry Onion Soup Mix
3. 1 Can Cream Of Mushroom Soup
4. 4-6 Medium Potatoes (peeled and quartered)

Place roast on large sheet of heavy duty foil. Mix soups and cover roast with soup mixture. Add potatoes and bring foil up and over roast. Roll and secure edges tightly, about 6-inches above roast. Bake. Serves 8-10.

NEW YORK ROAST BEEF

**Bake 350 Degrees
20 Minutes Per Pound**

1. 6-7 Pound Eye Of Round
2. 1 Tablespoon Oil
3. 1/2 Teaspoon Garlic Powder
4. 1 Teaspoon Ground Oregano

Rub oil all over roast. Combine garlic and oregano and rub over the oiled roast. Place in shallow baking pan with fat side up. Bake. Serves 10-12.

FLANK STEAK JOY

**Broil
6 Minutes Per Side**

1. 2 Pounds Lean Flank Steak
2. 2 Tablespoons Soy Sauce
3. 1 Tablespoon Sherry
4. 1 Teaspoon Honey

Mix soy, sherry and honey and marinate meat 4 hours or longer. Remove the steak from marinade and place on broiler pan. Broil. Slice across the grain into thin strips and serve. Serves 6-8.

MARINATED FLANK STEAK

Broil
8 Minutes Per Side

1.   Pounds Flank Steak
2.   1 Bottle (8 oz.) Italian Salad Dressing

Pour dressing over steak and marinate for 4 hours or longer. Broil. Slice across grain in thin strips. Serves 6-8.

TERRIYAKE MARINADE

Broil
10 Minutes Each Side

1.   2 Pounds Flank Steak
2.   1/3 Cup Soy Sauce
3.   1/3 Cup Pineapple Juice
4.   1/3 Cup Red Wine

Combine soy, pineapple and wine. Pour over flank steak and marinate 4 hours or longer. Broil. Serves 6-8.

SHERRIED BEEF   Bake 250 Degrees   3 Hours

1.   3 Pounds Lean Beef (cubed in 1 1/2-inch cubes)
2.   2 Cans Cream Of Mushroom Soup
3.   1/2 Cup Cooking Sherry
4.   1/2 Package Dry Onion Soup Mix

Mix all ingredients in casserole and bake covered. Serve this over rice or egg noodles. Serves 8.

ROUND STEAK BAKE   Bake 350 Degrees   1 1/2 Hours

1.   2 Pounds Round Steak
2.   4 Large Potatoes (peeled and quartered)
3.   2 Cans (6 oz. each) Mushrooms (not drained)
4.   1 Package Dry Onion Soup Mix

Place steak on foil and sprinkle soup mix on steak. Place potatoes evenly over steak and pour mushrooms with liquid over potatoes and steak. Wrap foil tightly. Bake. Serves 4-6.

BEEF STROGANOFF   Stove Top

1.   1 1/2 Pounds Round Steak (cut in 1/4-inch strips)
2.   2 Tablespoons Onion Soup Mix
3.   1 Can (6 oz.) Sliced Mushrooms
4.   1 Cup Sour Cream

Brown round steak in skillet. Add soup mix and can of mushrooms with liquid. Heat until bubbly. Slowly add sour cream and cook until thoroughly heated. Serve with noodles. Serves 4-6.

SWISS STEAK   Stove Top   1 1/2 Hours

1.   2 Pounds Round Steak
2.   1/2 Cup Flour
3.   1 Tablespoon Oil
4.   2 Cans (14 1/2 oz. each) Stewed Tomatoes

Flour steak and brown in oil. Remove from skillet and drain oil. Pour 1 can of tomatoes in skillet. Place steak on top and pour remaining can of tomatoes on steak. Cover and simmer. Serve with mashed potatoes. Serves 4-6.

BEEF IN WINE SAUCE   Stove Top   2 Hours

1.   3 Pounds Sirloin Steak (cut in 1/4-inch strips)
2.   2 Tablespoons Flour
3.   2 Cans Creamy Onion Soup
4.   2 Cups Burgundy Wine

Season meat to taste. Dredge strips in flour and brown in skillet. Add wine and soup and stir. Simmer covered. Serve with noodles. Serves 6-8.

BEEF GOULASH   Bake 350 Degrees   1 Hour

1.   2 Pounds Stew Beef
2.   1 Tablespoons Oil
3.   1 1/2 Cups Onion (chopped)
4.   1 Can Zesty Tomato Soup

Sauté meat and onion in oil. Add soup. Cover and place in oven. Bake. Serve with noodles. Serves 4-6.

HOT DOG STEW   Stove Top   25 Minutes

1.   1 Package Beef Hot Dogs (cut in 1/2-inch pieces)
2.   3 Medium Potatoes (peeled and diced)
3.   2 Tablespoons Flour
4.   1/2 Cup Water

Brown hot dogs in ungreased skillet. Add diced potatoes. Mix flour and water until smooth. Pour over hot dog and potato mixture. Salt and pepper to taste. Cover and simmer. Serves 4.

NEW ENGLAND DINNER   Stove Top   3 Hours

1.   4 Pounds Corned Beef
2.   1 Head Cabbage (cut into eights)
3.   8 Potatoes (peeled and halved)
4.   8 Carrots (peeled and halved)

Cover meat with cold water. Simmer 3 hours, adding the potatoes, carrots and cabbage the last hour. Drain and serve. Serves 8-10.

LIVER WITH APPLES AND ONIONS   Stove Top

1.   4 Slices Calf Liver (about 1 pound)
2.   4 Tablespoons Margarine
3.   3 Medium Onions (peeled and sliced)
4.   2 Apples (cored, cut into rings 1/2-inch thick)

Dry the liver. Sauté onions in 3 tablespoons margarine. Remove onion rings and sauté apples until they are cooked through, but not mushy (about 2-3 minutes on each side). Remove apples. Sauté liver about 2-3 minutes on each side. Place on platter and top with onions and apples. Serves 4.

SHERRY CHICKEN Bake 350 Degrees   1 Hour

1.   6 Medium Chicken Breasts (skinned and boned)
2.   1 Can Cream Of Mushroom Soup
3.   1 1/3 Cup Sour Cream
4.   1/2 Cup Cooking Sherry

Place chicken in greased baking dish. Combine remaining ingredients and pour over chicken. Bake. Serves 4-6.

COMPANY CHICKEN   Bake 350 Degrees   1 Hour

1.   6 Chicken Breasts (skinned and boned)
2.   1/4 Cup Sherry Or White Wine
3.   1/2 Cup Chicken Broth
4.   1/2 Cup Grated Parmesan Cheese

Place chicken in baking dish. Pour wine and broth on top of chicken. Sprinkle with Parmesan cheese. Bake covered 45 minutes and uncovered 15 minutes. Serve with white rice. Serves 4-6.

SOY SAUCE CHICKEN   Bake 350 Degrees   1 Hour
1.   4 Chicken Breasts (skinned and boned)
2.   1 Cup Sour Cream
3.   1/4 Cup Soy Sauce

Place chicken in greased casserole dish. Mix sour cream and soy sauce together. Spread over chicken. Bake covered. Serves 4.

CHICKEN DRIED BEEF   Bake 300 Degrees   2 Hours

1.   6 Chicken Breasts (skinned and boned)
2.   2 Jars (4 oz. each) Separated Sliced Dried Beef
3.   6 Strips Bacon
4.   1 Can Cream Of Mushroom Soup

Place dried beef in greased casserole. Wrap bacon strip around each chicken breast and place over beef. Spread soup over chicken; cover and bake. Serves 4-6.

CHICKEN DRIED BEEF II   Bake 275 Degrees   2 Hours

1.   1 Jar (4 oz.) Sliced Dried Beef (chopped)
2.   4 Chicken Breasts (skinned and boned)
3.   1 Cup Sour Cream
4.   1 Can Cream Of Mushroom Soup

Place dried beef in bottom of greased casserole and place chicken on top. Combine sour cream and soup; spread over chicken. Bake uncovered. Serves 4.

CHICKEN OREGANO   Bake 325 Degrees   1 1/2 Hours

1.   4 Chicken Breasts (skinned and boned)
2.   1 Tablespoon Oregano
3.   1 Teaspoon Garlic Salt
4.   1/2 Cup Margarine (melted)

Mix all ingredients except chicken. Pour over chicken and marinate at least 4 hours. Bake uncovered. Serves 4.

CHICKEN SUPREME   Bake 300 Degrees   1 1/2 Hours

1.   4 Chicken Breasts (skinned and boned)
2.   4 Slices Onion
3.   4-5 Potatoes (peeled and quartered)
4.   1 Can Golden Mushroom Soup

Line casserole with foil. Place chicken on foil. Top chicken with onion and place potatoes around chicken. Spread soup over potatoes and chicken. Seal foil tightly over chicken. Bake. Serves 4.

OVEN FRIED RITZ CHICKEN Bake 350 Degrees 1 Hour

1.   8 Chicken Breasts (skinned and boned)
2.   1/2 Box Ritz Crackers (crushed into fine crumbs)
3.   1/2 Cup Yogurt

Dip chicken in yogurt and roll in cracker crumbs. Place chicken in casserole dish and bake 30 minutes on each side. Serves 6-8.

BAKED CHICKEN PARMESAN   Bake 350 Degrees
                                                    1 Hour

1.   3 Pounds Chicken Pieces
2.   1 Cup Cornflake Crumbs
3.   1/2 Cup Grated Parmesan Cheese
4.   3/4 Cup Miracle Whip Salad Dressing

Combine crumbs and cheese. Brush chicken with salad dressing and coat with crumb mixture. Place in casserole dish and bake. Serves 4-6.

POTATO CHIP CHICKEN Bake 350 Degrees 1 Hour

1.   2-3 Pounds Chicken Pieces (remove skin)
2.   1 Cup Margarine (melted)
3.   2 Cups Crushed Potato Chips
4.   1/4 Teaspoon Garlic Salt

Mix crushed potato chips with garlic salt (flavored chips such as sour cream-onion can be used). Dip chicken in melted margarine and roll in potato chips. Place on baking sheet. Spread remaining margarine and chips over chicken. Bake. Serves 4-6.

CHICKEN SCALLOP Bake 350 Degrees 30 Minutes

1.   1 1/2 Cups Diced Cooked Chicken
2.   1 Package (6 oz.) Noodles
3.   2 Cups Chicken Gravy (see recipe below)
4.   1/2 Cup Buttered Crumbs

Prepare noodles as directed on package. Arrange alternate layers of noodles and chicken and gravy in greased baking dish. Cover with crumbs and bake. Serves 4.

QUICK CHICKEN GRAVY

1.   1 1/2 Tablespoons Flour
2.   1 Cup Milk
3.   1 Can Cream Of Chicken Soup

Blend flour and milk and add to soup. Heat slowly to boiling and cook until thickened.

CHICKEN DRESSING Bake 350 Degrees 45 Minutes

1.   1 Chicken
2.   1 Package (8 oz.) Corn Bread Stuffing Mix
3.   2 Cans Cream Of Chicken Mushroom Soup
4.   1/2 Cup Margarine (melted)

Boil chicken until meat separates from bone. Cool and debone. Retain 2 cups of broth. Mix melted margarine with stuffing mix. Dilute soup with 1 cup broth. Layer in large baking dish - beginning with dressing, then chicken, then soup. Repeat ending with dressing. Pour remaining 1 cup of broth over mixture. Bake uncovered. Serves 4-6.

CHICKEN RICE   Bake 350 Degrees   30 Minutes

1.   2 Cups Cooked Chicken (cut up)
2.   1 Box Uncle Bens Wild Rice Mix
3.   1 Can Cream Mushroom Soup
4.   1/2 Soup Can Milk

Mix all ingredients and pour in greased 2 quart dish. Cover and bake. Serves 4-6.

BUSY DAY CHICKEN   Bake 325 Degrees   2 Hours

1.   2-3 Pounds Chicken Pieces
2.   1 Cup Rice (uncooked)
3.   1 Package Dry Onion Soup Mix
4.   1 Can Cream Of Celery Soup

Place rice in greased casserole with chicken on top. Sprinkle with onion soup. Mix celery soup and two cans water; pour over the chicken. Bake covered. Serves 4-6.

CHICKEN DIJON   Bake 350 Degrees   1 Hour

1.   3 Pounds Chicken Pieces
2.   1/2 Cup Miracle Whip Salad Dressing
3.   1/4 Cup Dijon Mustard
4.   1 1/4 Cup Dry Bread Crumbs

Combine salad dressing and mustard. Coat chicken with mixture and crumbs. Bake. Serves 4-6.

CHICKEN SOUR CREAM Bake 350 Degrees   1 1/2 Hours

1.   3 Pounds Chicken Fryer (cut up)
2.   1 Carton (8 oz.) Sour Cream
3.   1 Package Dry Onion Soup Mix
4.   1/2 Cup Milk

Mix sour cream, soup and milk and pour over chicken. Cover and bake. Serves 4-6.

SWEET AND SOUR CHICKEN   Bake 350 Degrees
1 1/2 Hrs

1. 2-3 Pounds Chicken Pieces
2. 1 Package Dry Onion Soup Mix
3. 1 Jar (12 oz.) Apricot Preserves
4. 1 Bottle (8 oz.) Russian Salad Dressing

Place chicken in shallow baking pan. Mix remaining ingredients and pour on chicken. Bake. Serve with white rice. Serves 4-6.

LEMON BUTTER CHICKEN   Bake 350 Degrees
1 1/2 Hours

1. 2-3 Pounds Chicken Pieces
2. 1/2 Cup Margarine (melted)
3. 2 Lemons
4. 1/2 Teaspoon Garlic Salt

Rub chicken with lemon. Mix margarine, juice of one lemon and garlic salt. Pour over chicken and bake. Baste occasionally. Serves 4-6.

CHICKEN - CHICKEN SOUP   Bake 350 Degrees
1 1/2 Hours

1. 2-3 Pounds Chicken Pieces
2. 2 Cans Mushroom Chicken Soup
3. 1/2 Cup Milk
4. Parsley

Place chicken in large casserole. Mix soup and milk. Pour over chicken. Sprinkle with parsley. Bake. Serves 4-6.

GOLDEN CHICKEN Bake 400 Degrees   1 Hour

1.   2 Pounds Chicken Pieces
2.   2 Tablespoons Margarine
3.   1 Can Cream Of Chicken Soup
4.   1/2 Cup Sliced Almonds

Melt margarine in 9x13 baking dish. Arrange chicken in dish; bake for 40 minutes. Turn chicken and cover with soup. Sprinkle with almonds and bake 20 minutes longer. Serves 4-6.

ORANGE CHICKEN   Bake 350 Degrees
1 Hour 15 Minutes

1.   8 Pieces Of Chicken
2.   1 Cup Flour
3.   1 Can Frozen Orange Juice (thawed)
4.   1 Bunch Green Onions (chopped)

Dredge chicken pieces in flour; brown. Place in casserole. Cover with green onions and drizzle with juice. Cover and bake 1 hour; uncover and continue to bake for 15 minutes. Serves 4-6.

WORCHESTER CHICKEN   Bake 350 Degrees   1 Hour

1.   2-3 Pounds Chicken Pieces
2.   1/4 Cup Worcestershire Sauce
3.   1/2 Cup Margarine
4.   2 Tablespoons Lemon Pepper

Place chicken in large greased casserole. Spread margarine on each piece of chicken. Sprinkle with lemon pepper and Worcestershire. Bake. Serves 4-6.

MUSHROOM CHICKEN   Bake 350 Degrees   1 1/2 Hours

1.   6 Chicken Breasts, Thighs Or Legs
2.   3 Tablespoons Oil
3.   2 (4 oz. each) Cans Button Mushrooms
4.   2 Cans Cream Of Mushroom Soup

Brown chicken in oil in frying pan. Remove and arrange chicken in casserole. Combine soup and mushrooms and pour over chicken. Bake. Serves 4-6.

LEMON PEPPER CHICKEN Bake 350 Degrees   1 Hour

1.   2-3 Pounds Chicken Pieces
2.   4 Tablespoons Margarine (melted)
3.   1/2 Cup Soy Sauce
4.   Lemon Pepper

Place chicken in greased baking dish. Spread margarine, soy sauce and lemon pepper on each piece of chicken. Bake. Serves 4-6.

MARINATED CHICKEN   Broil 20 Minutes Per Side

1.   2 Broiling Chickens
2.   3/4 Cup Olive Oil
3.   1 Clove Garlic (finely chopped)
4.   1/2 Cup Chopped Parsley

Split chicken down the back. Combine oil, garlic and parsley; marinate chicken for minimum of 1/2 hour or overnight. Arrange marinated chickens, skin side up, on preheated broiler 5-inches from heat. Broil 20 minutes per side. Baste regularly. Serves 6-8.

ITALIAN BROILED CHICKEN   Broil 16 Minutes
Bake 350 20 Minutes

1.   1 Fryer Chicken (quartered)
2.   1/2 Cup Margarine
3.   3 Tablespoons Lemon Juice
4.   1 Package Italian Salad Dressing Mix

Melt margarine in frying pan and add lemon juice and salad mix. Dip chicken in this mixture and place, skin side up, on rack in broiler pan. Broil 8 minutes per side. Change oven setting to 350 and pour remaining butter mixture over chicken. Bake uncovered at 350 for 20 minutes. Serves 4-6.

CHICKEN CACCIATORE   **Stove Top**

1.   2 1/2 Pounds Chicken Pieces
2.   1 Medium Onion (chopped)
3.   1 Jar (14 oz.) Spaghetti Sauce
4.   1/2 Teaspoon Dried Basil

Brown chicken pieces skin side down over low heat. Cook chicken 10 minutes each side. Sauté onions until soft. Stir in sauce and basil. Cover and simmer 20 minutes. Serve with spaghetti. Serves 4-6.

CHICKEN LIVERS AND MUSHROOMS   **Stove Top**

1.   1 Pound Chicken Livers
2.   2 Tablespoons Oil
3.   1 Large Can (6 oz.) Whole Mushrooms
4.   1/2 Cup Red Wine

Sauté livers slowly in oil. Add red wine and mushrooms. Heat. Serve over rice. Serves 4.

SWINGING WINGS   Bake 350 Degrees   1 Hour

1.   10 Chicken Wings
2.   1/2 Cup Margarine (melted)
3.   1 Small Box Parmesan Cheese
4.   1 Teaspoon Garlic Powder

Dip wings in margarine and then in combined mixture of cheese and garlic powder. Place in casserole and bake. Serves 4.

CORNISH HENS   Bake 350 Degrees   1 Hour

1.   4 Cornish Hens
2.   4 Tablespoons Margarine
3.   1/2 Cup Water
4.   2 Tablespoons Soy Sauce

Rub hens with margarine. Place in greased baking dish and spoon water and soy sauce mixture over hem. Cover with foil and bake for 45 minutes. Remove cover and bake 15 minutes longer. Serves 4.

SWEET SOUR PORK CHOPS Bake 350 Degrees   I Hour

1.   6-8 Thick Pork Chops
2.   1/4 Cup Soy Sauce
3.   1/4 Cup Chili Sauce
4.   1/4 Cup Honey

Mix honey, soy, and chili sauces. Place pork chops in greased 3 quart casserole. Pour mixture over chops. Bake. Serves 6-8.

HAWAIIAN PORK CHOPS   Stove Top   1 1/2 Hours

1.   4 Loin Pork Chops
2.   1/4 Cup Flour
3.   2 Tablespoons Oil
4.   4 Slices Canned Pineapple (reserve 1/3 cup juice)

Dredge chops in flour. Brown in skillet with oil. Top each chop with a ring of pineapple. Add pineapple juice. Cover and cook slowly. Remove meat and pineapple to platter. Pour the remaining juice over chops. Serves 4.

HAWAIIAN BAKED PORK

Bake 350 Degrees For 1 Hour
Bake 450 Degrees For 10 Minutes

1.   4 Pork Chops
2.   2 Cups Crushed Pineapple
3.   3 Medium Sweet Potatoes (peeled, sliced)
4.   2 Tablespoons Brown Sugar

Place pineapple with juice in large greased baking dish. Place sliced sweet potatoes over pineapple and sprinkle with brown sugar. Place pork chops on top of sweet potatoes. Bake covered 350 degrees for 1 hour; uncovered 450 degrees for 10 minutes. Serves 4.

PORK CHOP SCALLOP   Stove Top   45 Minutes

1.   4 Pork Chops (1/2-inch thick)
2.   1 Package Scalloped Potatoes
3.   2 Tablespoons Margarine
4.   Milk (amount called for in box of potatoes)

In skillet brown chops in margarine. Remove chops and set aside. Empty potatoes and packet of seasoned sauce mix into skillet. Stir in water and milk called for on package. Heat to boiling, reduce heat and place chops on top. Cover and simmer 35 minutes or until potatoes are tender and chops are thoroughly done. Serves 4.

PORK POTATO CASSEROLE
Bake 350 Degrees - 1 Hour
Bake 375 Degrees - 1/2 Hour

1.   4-6 Pork Chops
2.   4-5 Potatoes (peeled and sliced 1/2-inch slices)
3.   1 Can Cheddar Cheese Soup
4.   1/2 Can Milk

Place two layers of potatoes in bottom of a greased casserole dish. Place pork chops on top. Combine soup and milk. Pour over chops. Bake 1 hour covered 350 degrees; uncovered 30 minutes at 375 degrees. Serves 4-6.

SAUSAGE CASSEROLE   Bake 400 Degrees   25 Minutes

1.   1 Pound Bulk Pork Sausage
2.   2 Cans (15 oz. each) Beans With Spicy Sauce
3.   1 Can (14 1/2 oz.) Diced Tomatoes (drained)
4.   1 Package Corn Muffin Mix

Brown sausage, drain fat. Add beans and tomatoes and blend. Bring to a boil. Pour into a 2 1/2 quart greased casserole. Prepare muffin mix according to package. Drop by spoonfuls over meat and bean mixture. Bake 25 minutes or until top is browned. Serves 4-6.

QUICKIE HAWAIIAN PORK   Stove Top   1 Hour

1.   2 Pound Lean Pork Roast (cut in 1-inch cubes)
2.   1 Can (14 oz.) Pineapple Chunks With Juice
3.   1/4 Cup Vinegar
4.   1 Teaspoon Ginger

Combine meat, pineapple with juice, vinegar and ginger.
Simmer one hour covered. Serve over rice. Serves 6.

ROAST PORK IN MARINADE Bake 350 Degrees 3 Hours

1.   4-6 Pound Lean Pork Roast
2.   1 Can (15 oz.) Tomatoes (chopped)
3.   1/4 Cup White Vinegar
4.   1/4 Cup Water

Place roast in roasting pan. Mix and pour the remaining
ingredients over roast. Best marinated overnight. Cover and
bake. Serves 8-10.

SUNDAY HAM   Bake 300 Degrees   3 Hours

1.   2-3 Pounds Boneless Smoked Ham
2.   1/4 Cup Prepared Mustard
3.   1/4 Cup Brown Sugar
4.   4 Potatoes (peeled and quartered)

Place ham in roaster. Combine mustard and sugar. Spread
over ham. Place potatoes around ham. Cover and bake.
Serves 8-10.

PORK CASSEROLE Bake 325 Degrees   4 Hours

1.   2 Pounds Lean Pork (cut into 1-inch cubes)
2.   2 Large Cans (16 oz. each) Sauerkraut (drained)
3.   2 Medium Onions (sliced)
4.   3 Cups Water

Brown pork in skillet and set aside. Spread 1/2 sauerkraut in 2 quart greased casserole. Cover with 1 onion. Place pork on top. Layer onions and sauerkraut on top of pork. Pour water over all, cover and bake. Serves 6.

SPARERIBS SAUERKRAUT Bake 350 Degrees   1 Hour

1.   4 Pounds Spareribs
2.   2 Large Cans (16 oz. each) Sauerkraut
3.   1/4 Cup Brown Sugar
4.   1/2 Cup Hot Water

Place sauerkraut in greased casserole and sprinkle with brown sugar. Place spareribs on sauerkraut. Add hot water, cover and bake. Serves 4.

BARBECUED SPARERIBS Bake 350 Degrees   2 Hours

1.   4 Pounds Spareribs
2.   2 Medium Onions (sliced)
3.   1 Bottle (18 oz.) Barbecue Sauce

Place ribs in roaster. Add onions. Pour sauce over ribs and cook covered for 1 1/2 hours. Remove cover and cook 30 minutes longer. Serves 4.

PORK TENDERLOIN   Bake 325 Degrees   5 Hours

1.   3 Pounds Pork Tenderloin
2.   1 Can (15 oz.)Tomato Sauce
3.   1 Package Dry Onion Soup Mix
4.   2 Tablespoons Worcestershire Sauce

Place tenderloin strips on aluminum foil. Mix remaining ingredients; spread over meat. Seal foil and place in shallow pan. Bake. Cut meat into 1-inch slices. Pour gravy in pan over slices of meat. Serves 6-8.

CRANBERRY HAM   Bake 300 Degrees   1 Hour

1.   1 Slice Ham (2-inches thick)
2.   1 Cup Whole Cranberry Sauce
3.   2 Tablespoons Brown Sugar
4.   1/4 Teaspoon Cloves

Place ham in greased casserole. Spoon cranberry sauce evenly over ham. Sprinkle with brown sugar and cloves. Bake covered. Serves 4.

BROILED TROUT   Broil   13 Minutes

1.   2 Pounds Fish Fillets
2.   2 Tablespoons Onion (grated)
3.   2 Large Tomatoes (cut into small pieces)
4.   1 Cup Swiss Cheese (grated)

Place fillets in greased casserole. Sprinkle onion and tomatoes over fillets. Broil 10 minutes. Sprinkle with cheese and
broil another 3 minutes.
Serves 4.

TUNA CHIP CASSEROLE   Bake 375 Degrees
                                    30 Minutes

1.   1 Can (6 1/2 oz.) Tuna (drained)
2.   1 Can (10 3/4 oz.) Cream Of Mushroom Soup
3.   3/4 Cup Milk
4.   1 Cup Crushed Potato Chips

Break chunks of tuna into a bowl. Stir in soup and milk. Add
3/4 cup crushed potato chips. Mix well. Pour into greased
baking dish. Sprinkle the remaining chips over top. Bake.
Serves 4-6.

HERBED SALMON STEAKS

**Bake 450 Degrees
45 Minutes**

1.   3 Packages (12 oz. each) Frozen Salmon Steaks
2.   1/4 Cup Lemon Juice
3.   2 Teaspoons Marjoram Leaves
4.   2 Teaspoons Onion Salt

Place frozen fish in greased casserole. Mix lemon juice, marjoram leaves and onion salt. Spoon on fish and bake. Serves 4-6.

SALMONETTES

Stove Top

1.   1 Can (15 oz.) Pink Salmon (drained, flaked)
2.   1 Egg
3.   1/2 Cup Bisquick Mix
4.   1/2 Cup Oil

Mix salmon and egg in bowl. Add biscuit mix and stir. Heat oil in skillet and drop salmon mixture by tablespoonfuls into skillet. Flatten each salmonette with spatula. Cook each side until brown, around 2-3 minutes per side. Serves 4.

SERVING IDEA - Lemon Butter Sauce is complimentary to many hot fish entrees. To make, cream 1/2 cup softened butter and gradually add 3 tablespoons lemon juice.

SCALLOPED OYSTERS   **Bake 350 Degrees**

1.   1 Pint Oysters
2.   2 Cups Fine Cracker Crumbs
3.   4 Tablespoons Margarine
4.   1 Can Condensed Chicken Gumbo Soup

Drain and reserve liquid from oysters. Place one layer oysters in large baking dish; season to taste and cover with layer of crumbs and half of soup mixture. Repeat layers. Dot with margarine and bake until edges of oysters curl and top is browned. Serves 4.

ITALIAN SHRIMP   **Stove Top**   **10 Minutes**

1.   3 Pounds Raw Shrimp (peeled and cleaned)
2.   1/2 Pound Margarine
3.   12 Ounces Italian Dressing
4.   Juice Of Two Lemons

Melt margarine and mix dressing and lemon juice in skillet. Stir in shrimp. Sauté for 10 minutes, turning occasionally. Serves 4-6.

SCALLOPS AND BACON Bake 475 Degrees   20 Minutes

1.   1 Pound Scallops
2.   3 Tablespoons Margarine
3.   8 slices Bacon
4.   Salt And Pepper

Cook scallops in margarine 5 minutes. Cut bacon into 2-inch pieces. Arrange bacon and scallops alternately on skewer. Sprinkle with salt and pepper. To bake, insert skewers in uncooked potato halves, so they will stand upright. Bake. Serves 4.

CRAB ROLL   Bake 400 Degrees   30 Minutes

1.   1 Can (6 oz.) Crab
2.   1 Can Refrigerator Biscuits
3.   1 Small Onion (chopped)
4.   Mayonnaise

Roll biscuit dough to 1/4-inch thick on floured board. Combine crab and onion and moisten slightly with mayonnaise. Mix and spread on dough. Roll this dough and mixture into a jellyroll and cut into 1 1/2-inch slices. Bake on greased baking sheet. Serves 4-6.

CRABMEAT CASSEROLE Bake 350 Degrees 30 Minutes

1.   1 Pound Crabmeat or Imitation Crabmeat
2.   1 Can (2.8 oz.) Durkees Fried Onions
3.   1 Can Cream Of Mushroom Soup
4.   3/4 Cup Cracker Crumbs

Mix all ingredients. Place in buttered casserole dish. Bake.
Serves 4-6.

SEAFOOD CASSEROLE Bake 400 Degrees   30 Minutes

1. 1/4 Pound Crabmeat (flaked)
2. 1/4 Pound Shrimp (peeled and cleaned)
3. 1/4 Pound Scallops
4. 1 Can Cheddar Cheese Soup

Mix fish ingredients and place in greased casserole dish.
Cover with soup and bake. Serve with rice. Serves 4.

DESSERTS

PIE SHELL

1.   1 Cup Flour
2.   1/2 Teaspoon Salt
3.   1/3 Cup Shortening
4.   2-3 Tablespoons Ice Water

Combine flour and salt. Cut shortening into dry ingredients until mixture resembles corn meal. Add ice water one tablespoon at a time. Stir with fork. Form into a ball. Place on lightly floured surface and roll from center to edge until 1/8-inch thick. Makes one-9-inch pie shell.

PAT IN PAN CRUST

1.   2 Cups Flour
2.   2/3 Cup Margarine
3.   1/2 Cup Chopped Nuts (almonds or pecans)
4.   1/2 Cup Powdered Sugar

Mix ingredients. Press firmly into ungreased pie plate. Makes two 9-inch pie shells. Bake 15 minutes at 350 degrees.

NUT CRUST

1.   1/4 Cup Margarine (softened)
2.   1/4 Cup Sugar
3.   1 Tablespoon Flour
4.   1 Cup Pecans (ground)

Combine all ingredients. Press over bottom and sides of greased 9-inch pie plate. Bake 10 minutes at 325 degrees. Cool.

GRAHAM CRACKER CRUST

1.   1 1/2 Cups Graham Cracker Crumbs
2.   2 Tablespoons Sugar
3.   6 Tablespoons Margarine (melted)

Combine all ingredients and press evenly into a 9-inch pie plate. Bake 10 minutes at 350 degrees. Cool.

CHOCOLATE PIE SHELL

1.   1 1/4 Cups Chocolate Wafer Crumbs
2.   1/4 Cup Margarine (melted)
3.   2 Tablespoons Sugar
4.   1/4 Teaspoon Cinnamon

Combine all ingredients and press onto bottom of greased 9-inch pie plate. Bake 8 minutes at 375 degrees.

MERINGUE SHELL

1.   4 Egg Whites (room temperature)
2.   1/2 Teaspoon Cream of Tartar
3.   1 1/2 Cups Sugar
4.   1 Teaspoon Vanilla

Beat egg whites until foamy. Add cream of tartar and beat until stiff. Gradually add sugar and vanilla. Spoon meringue into 9-inch pie pan so that it covers bottom and sides. Bake 1 hour at 275 degrees. Let cool in oven. Great for fruit or cream fillings.

APPLE CREAM PIE - Unbaked Pie Shell

1.   4 Cups Apples (peeled and diced)
2.   1 Cup Sugar
3.   1 Cup Half And Half
4.   2 Tablespoons Flour

Combine all ingredients. Pour into unbaked pie shell. Bake 45 minutes to 1 hour or until brown at 350 degrees.

BOURBON PIE - Baked Chocolate Pie Shell

1.   21 Large Marshmallows
2.   1 Can (12 oz.) Evaporated Milk
3.   1 Cup Whipping Cream
4.   3 Tablespoons Bourbon

Combine marshmallows and canned milk in saucepan. Cook over low heat, stirring constantly, until all the marshmallows have melted. Chill completely. Whip cream and fold in marshmallow mixture and bourbon. Pour into pie shell and chill 4-6 hours.

COCONUT PIE - Unbaked Pie Shell

1.   3 Eggs
2.   1/4 Cup Buttermilk
3.   2/3 Cup Butter (melted)
4.   2 Cups (7 oz.) Flaked Coconut

Mix all ingredients and pour into pie shell. Bake 45 minutes at 350 degrees.

CARAMEL BOX PIE - Baked Nut Crust

1.   1 Can (14 oz.) Sweetened Condensed Milk
2.   1 Large Banana (peeled and sliced)
3.   1 Carton (8 oz.) Cool Whip
4.   2 (1.4 oz. each) Skor Bars (chilled and crushed)

Pour sweetened condensed milk into a non-stick skillet over medium-low heat. Cook for 10-12 minutes, stirring frequently. Milk will thicken and turn caramel color. Remove from heat. Cool. Place sliced bananas in 9-inch nut crust and spread caramelized milk over bananas. Spoon Cool Whip on top and sprinkle with crushed candy. Refrigerate.

QUICK CHEESE CAKE PIE - Graham Cracker Crust

1.   1 Package (8 oz.) Cream Cheese (softened)
2.   2 Cups Whole Milk
3.   1 Package (3 1/2 oz.) Lemon Instant Pudding Mix

Blend softened cream cheese and 1 1/2 cup of the milk. Add remaining milk and pudding mix. Beat slowly just until well mixed, about 1 minute...do not overbeat! Pour at once into graham cracker crust. Chill 1 hour.

CHEESECAKE - Unbaked Graham Cracker Crust

1.   3 Packages (8 oz. each) Cream Cheese
2.   1 Cup Sugar
3.   5 Eggs
4.   1 1/2 Teaspoon Vanilla

Cream the cream cheese and eggs, adding one egg at a time. Add sugar and vanilla. Pour into graham cracker crust and bake 1 hour at 350 degrees, or until center is set.

LAZY CHOCOLATE ICEBOX PIE - Baked Pie Shell

1.   20 Large Marshmallows
2.   1 (8 oz.) Almond Chocolate Bar
3.   1 Carton (8 oz.) Cool Whip
4.   Pecans (chopped)

Melt marshmallows and chocolate over low heat or double boiler. Cool partially and fold in Cool Whip. Place in pie shell. Sprinkle with pecans if desired. Chill.

LEMONADE PIE - Baked Graham Cracker Crust

1.   1 Can (14 oz.) Sweetened Condensed Milk
2.   1 Can (6 oz.) Frozen Lemonade (thawed)
3.   1 Carton (8 oz.) Cool Whip

Combine and mix all ingredients. Do not beat. Place in pie shell and freeze.

COOKIE CREAM PIE -Baked Chocolate Pie Shell

1.   1 1/2 Cup Cold Half And Half
2.   1 Package (3 1/2 oz.) Jello Instant Vanilla Pudding
3.   1 Carton (8 oz.) Cool Whip
4.   1 Cup Crushed Chocolate Sandwich Cookies

Pour half and half into large bowl. Add pudding mix. Beat at low speed until well blended, about 1 minute. Let stand 5 minutes. Fold in Cool Whip and crushed cookies. Pour into baked pie shell. Freeze about 6 hours. Remove and let stand 10 minutes before serving.

MISSISSIPPI MUD PIE - Baked Chocolate Pie Shell

1.   1 1/2 Cups Half And Half
2.   1 Package (3 1/2 oz.) Instant Vanilla Pudding
3.   1 Tablespoon Instant Coffee
4.   1 Carton (8 oz.) Cool Whip

Pour half and half into large bowl. Add pudding mix. Beat at low speed until well blended, about 1 minute. Let stand 5 minutes and fold in instant coffee and Cool Whip. Place in pie shell. Freeze about 6 hours. Remove and let stand 10 minutes before serving.

MILLIONAIRE PIE - Baked Pie Shell

1 Cup Sugar
1 Package (8 oz.) Cream Cheese (softened)
3.   1 Can (15 1/4 oz.) Crushed Pineapple (drained)
4.   1 Carton (8 oz.) Cool Whip

Cream sugar with the cream cheese. Add drained pineapple. Fold in Cool Whip until well blended. Place in pie shell. Refrigerate. Serve cold.

PEACH PIE - Baked Pie Shell

1.   7 Peaches (peeled, sliced)
2.   1/4 Cup Sugar
3.   2 Tablespoons Cornstarch
4.   2 Tablespoons Margarine

Place all ingredients in pan and cook on stove top until thick and clear. Cool. Place in pie shell. Refrigerate.

PINEAPPLE PIE - Baked Graham Cracker Crust

1.   1 Can (14 oz.) Sweetened Condensed Milk
2.   1/2 Cup Lemon Juice
3.   1 Can (20 oz.) Crushed Pineapple (drained)
4.   1 Carton (8 oz.) Cool Whip

Combine milk and lemon juice. Stir well. Fold in pineapple and Cool Whip. Spoon into graham cracker crust. Chill.

PEACH YOGURT PIE - Baked Graham Cracker Crust

1. 1 Can (8 3/4 oz.) Sliced Peaches
2. 2 Containers (8 oz. each) Fruit Flavored Yogurt
3. 1 Carton (8 oz.) Cool Whip

Combine fruit and yogurt, then fold in Cool Whip, blending well. Spoon into graham cracker crust. Freeze until firm, about 4 hours. Remove from freezer and place in refrigerator 30 minutes before serving.

PECAN PIE - Unbaked Pie Shell

1. 3 Eggs (beaten)
2. 1 Cup Sugar
3. 3/4 Cup White Corn Syrup
4. 1 Cup Chopped Pecans

Mix all ingredients and place in pie shell. Bake 1 hour at 325 degrees or until inserted knife comes out clean.

COCKTAIL PIE - Baked Meringue Shell

1. 2 Cups Sour Cream
2. 1/2 Cup Sugar
3. 1 Teaspoon Vanilla
4. 1 Can (30 oz.) Fruit Cocktail (well drained)

Combine sour cream, sugar and vanilla. Fold in drained fruit cocktail. Place in cooled meringue shell. Refrigerate.

PUMPKIN PIE - Unbaked Pie Shell

1. 1 Can (16 oz.) Pumpkin
2. 1 Can (12 oz.) Sweetened Condensed Milk
3. 2 Eggs
4. 1 Teaspoon Pumpkin Pie Spice

Combine all ingredients and mix well. Pour into pie shell. Bake 15 minutes at 425 degrees; then reduce heat and bake 35-40 minutes longer at 350 degrees.

STRAWBERRY PIE - Baked Graham Cracker Crust

1. 1 Box (3 oz.) Strawberry Jello
2. 2/3 Cup Boiling Water And 2 Cups Ice Cubes
3. 1 Carton (8 oz.) Cool Whip
4. 1 Cup Sliced Strawberries

Dissolve jello in boiling water. Stir jello about 3 minutes; add 2 cups ice cubes. Stir until ice melts and jell-o thickens. Blend Cool Whip into jello until smooth. Fold in strawberries. Chill until mixture will mound. Spoon into graham cracker crust. Refrigerate at least 2 hours before serving.

MANDARIN CAKE (See Frosting Below)

1. 1 Package Yellow Cake Mix
2. 4 Eggs
3. 1 Can (11 oz.) Mandarin Oranges (reserve liquid)
4. 3/4 Cup Vegetable Oil

Pour 1 cup liquid from mandarin oranges into measuring cup. If there is not enough to make 1 cup, add water. Chop oranges. Mix all remaining ingredients with mandarin liquid. Pour into 3 greased pans lined with wax paper. Bake 20-25 minutes at 350 degrees.

MANDARIN CAKE FROSTING

1. 1 Can (20 oz.) Crushed Pineapple With Juice
2. 1 Package (3 1/2 oz.) Vanilla Pudding Mix
3. 1 Carton (12 oz.) Cool Whip

Mix all ingredients and frost cake. Refrigerate.

CHERRY PIE CAKE

1. 2 Cans (21 oz.) Cherry Pie Filling
2. 1/2 Cup Pecans (chopped)
3. 1 Box Yellow Cake Mix
4. 1/2 Cup Margarine

Mix cake with margarine to look like crumbled pie crust. Save 1 cup for topping. Spread rest in bottom of 9x12-inch greased pan. Pour pie filling on top. Put remaining "pie crust" and pecans on top. Bake 45 minutes at 350 degrees.

APPLE-CARROT CAKE (See Frosting Below)

1.   1 Package Carrot Cake Mix
2.   2/3 Cup Vegetable Oil
3.   3 Eggs
4.   1 Cup Apple Sauce

Combine mix, oil and eggs. Beat at medium speed for 3 minutes. Add applesauce and beat 1 minute. Pour into greased and floured tube pan. Bake 35 minutes at 350 degrees.

APPLE-CARROT GLAZE

1.   1 Package (4 oz.) Cream Cheese (softened)
2.   1 Cup Powdered Sugar
3.   3 Tablespoons Lemon Juice

Beat cream cheese until fluffy. Add sugar and lemon juice until smooth. Spread over warm cake.

REAL FRUIT CAKE

1.   1 1/2 Pound Candied Fruit (mixed)
2.   1 Can (3 1/2 oz.) Coconut
3.   1 Pound Pecan Pieces
4.   1 Can (14 oz.) Sweetened Condensed Milk

Mix all ingredients and spread in greased 5x9-inch loaf pan. Bake 2 hours at 250 degrees.

FLOP CAKE (See Frosting Below)

1. 2 Cups Flour
2. 2 Teaspoons Baking Soda
3. 1 1/2 Cups Sugar
4. 1 Can (20 oz.) Crushed Pineapple

Combine flour, soda and sugar. Add pineapple and mix well. Pour into greased and floured 9x13-inch pan. Bake 20-30 minutes at 350 degrees.

FLOP CAKE FROSTING

1. 1 Can (14 oz.) Sweetened Condensed Milk
2. 1/2 Cup Margarine (melted)
3. 1/2 Teaspoon Vanilla
4. 1 Cup Flaked Coconut

Combine milk and margarine and bring to a boil. Stirring constantly, boil for 4 minutes. Add coconut and mix. Spread over cake while it is hot.

CHOCOLATE POUND CAKE

1. 1 Package Chocolate Cake Mix
2. 1/2 Cup Oil
3. 1 1/4 Cup Water
4. 4 Eggs

Blend all ingredients and beat at medium speed for 2 minutes. Pour into greased and floured tube pan. Bake 1 hour at 350 degrees.

LEMON CAKE (see glaze below)

1. 1 Package Lemon Pudding Cake Mix
2. 2/3 Cup Oil
3. 4 Eggs
4. 1 1/4 Cups 7-Up

Mix cake and oil. Beat. Add eggs one at a time. Add 7-Up and beat. Pour into a greased and floured 13x9-inch cake pan. Bake at 350 degrees for 30 minutes.

LEMON CAKE GLAZE

1. 1/2 Cup Margarine (melted)
2. 2 Cups Powdered Sugar
3. 6-7 Tablespoons Lemon Lime-Soda
4. 1/2 Teaspoon Lemon Extract

Combine and spread over warm cake.

TIME SAVING IDEA - When you are in the mood to bake, prepare two cakes, one to serve now and one to freeze for later. Allow the cake for the freezer to cool. Pack in plastic freezer bags either whole or sliced. Freeze for up to six months. We prefer to frost our cakes the day we plan on serving them.

FRUIT COCKTAIL BREAD PUDDING

(See Sauce Below)

1.   4 Cups Flour
2.   2 Cups Sugar
3.   2 Teaspoons Baking Soda
4.   1 Can (30 oz.) Fruit Cocktail (undrained)

Mix all ingredients with a spoon. Pour into a greased and floured tube pan. Bake at 1 hour at 325°.

BREAD PUDDING SAUCE

1.   1 Cup Sugar
2.   1 Can (12 oz) Evaporated Milk
3.   1/2 Cup Butter
4.   1 Teaspoon Vanilla

Cook all ingredients over medium heat approximately 5 minutes. Spoon half over warm cake and use remaining for additional sauce when serving.

PREPARATION IDEA - Save the wrappers from margarine or butter in a ziplock bag in the refrigerator. When a recipe calls for a greased pan, use the wrappers to grease the pan.

STRAWBERRY CAKE (See Frosting Below)

1.   1 Package Strawberry Cake Mix
2.   3/4 Cup Water
3.   3 Eggs
4.   1 Can (8 1/4 oz.) Crushed Pineapple (save 1/4 cup liquid)

Mix all ingredients including 1/4 cup reserved liquid. Pour into a 9x13-inchgreased and floured pan. Bake 45-55 minutes at 350 degrees.

STRAWBERRY CAKE FROSTING

1.   1 Package (3 1/2 oz.) Vanilla Instant Pudding Mix
2.   1 Cup Milk
3.   1 Cup Whipping Cream
4.   1 Teaspoon Almond Flavoring

Mix pudding and milk. Set aside. Beat whipping cream with flavoring until stiff. Fold pudding mixture and whip cream mixture together. Frost cake. Refrigerate.

Occasionally check your oven for temperature accuracy. We recommend investing in a good oven thermometer.

CHOCOLATE CHIP COOKIES

1.   1 Package Yellow Cake Mix
2.   1/2 Cup Oil
3.   2 Eggs
4.   1 Package (6 oz.) Semi-Sweet Chocolate Chips

Mix all ingredients. Drop by teaspoonful on lightly greased cookie sheet. Bake 10 minutes at 375 degrees.

COCONUT CHOCOLATE COOKIES

1.   1 Package Chocolate Cake Mix
2.   1 Cup Flaked Coconut
3.   2 Eggs
4.   1/2 Cup Oil

Mix all ingredients. Place mixture in greased and floured 15x10x1-inch pan. Bake 15-20 minutes at 350 degrees. Cool and cut into bars.

QUICK COOKIES

1.   1/4 Cup Brown Sugar
2.   1/2 Cup Margarine (softened)
3.   1 Cup Flour
4.   1 Teaspoon Vanilla

Mix all ingredients and form into 1-inch balls. Place on cookie sheet and bake 10 minutes at 350 degrees.

PRALINE SHORTBREAD COOKIES

1. 1 Cup Butter (softened)
2. 3/4 Cup Packed Brown Sugar
3. 1 1/2 Cup Flour
4. 1/2 Cup Ground Pecans

Cream butter and add sugar. Beat at medium speed until light and fluffy. Stir in flour and pecans...dough will be stiff. Press onto bottom of greased and floured 15x10x1-inch pan. Score into 2-inch squares. Bake 20 minutes at 325 degrees. Break into wedges.

SHORTBREAD COOKIES

1. 1 Cup Butter (softened)
2. 3/4 Cup Powdered Sugar
3. 1/4 Cup Cornstarch
4. 1 3/4 Cup Flour

Cream butter; gradually add powdered sugar and corn starch. Beat until light and fluffy. Add flour. Press into lightly greased and floured 15x10x1-inch pan. Bake 30-35 minutes at 325 degrees. Cut into squares while warm.

SHORTBREAD

1. 1 Cup Butter (softened)
2. 1/2 Cup Powdered Sugar (sifted)
3. 2 Cups Flour
4. Sugar

Cream butter. Add powdered sugar, beating until light and fluffy. Stir in flour...mixture will be stiff. Press onto bottom of greased and floured 15 x 10 x1 -inch pan. Prick all over with a fork. Chill 30 minutes. Bake 5 minutes at 375 degrees. Reduce heat to 300 degrees and bake 25 minutes or until golden brown. Cut into 1 1/2-inch squares while warm. Sprinkle with sugar.

PRALINE GRAHAM COOKIES

1. 1 Package Graham Crackers
2. 1 Cup Butter
3. 11/2 Cups Brown Sugar
4. 2 Cups Pecans (chopped)

Put crackers in single layer on 15x10x1-inch pan. Boil butter, sugar and pecans for 2 minutes, stirring constantly. Spread on graham crackers. Bake 10 minutes at 350 degrees.

WALNUT/SPICE COOKIES

1. 1/4 Cup Sugar
2. 1 Teaspoon Pumpkin Pie Spice Seasoning
3. 1 Egg White (room temperature)
4. 1 Cup Walnuts (finely chopped)

Mix sugar and seasoning. Beat egg white on high for 1 minute. Gradually add sugar mixture. Beat until stiff. Fold in walnuts. Drop onto greased cookie sheet. Bake 35-40 minutes at 250 degrees.

SWEET CEREAL PUFFS

1. 3 Egg Whites
2. 2/3 Cup Sugar
3. 4 Cups Total Cereal

Beat egg whites to a foam. Add sugar gradually, beating until stiff. Fold in cereal. Drop 2-inches apart on greased cookie sheet. Bake 14 minutes or until brown at 325 degrees. Cool.

PEANUT BUTTER COOKIES I - No Bake

1.   1 Cup Sugar
2.   1 Cup Corn Syrup
3.   1 Jar (12 oz.) Crunchy Peanut Butter
4.   5 Cups Crisp Rice Cereal

Melt sugar and corn syrup. Add peanut butter, cereal; mix.
Form into 1-inch balls. Place on wax paper. Cool.

PEANUT BUTTER COOKIES II

1.   1 Cup Crunchy Peanut Butter
2.   1 Egg
3.   1 Cup Sugar
4.   1 Teaspoon Vanilla

Mix all ingredients and form into 1-inch balls. Press flat on
greased cookie sheet with a fork. Bake 10 minutes at 350
degrees.

EASY PEANUT BUTTER COOKIES

1.   1 Can (14 oz.) Sweetened Condensed Milk
2.   3/4 Cup Peanut Butter
3.   2 Cups Biscuit Mix
4.   1 Teaspoon Vanilla Extract

Beat milk and peanut butter until smooth. Add biscuit mix
and vanilla and mix well. Shape into 1-inch balls. Place 2-
inches apart on ungreased baking sheet. Flatten with fork.
Bake 6-8 minutes at 375 degrees.

PEANUT BUTTER FUDGE

1.   1 Cup Peanut Butter
2.   1 Cup Corn Syrup
3.   1 1/4 Cups Non-fat Dry Milk
4.   1 1/4 Cups Confectioners Sugar

Mix all ingredients and stir until well blended. Knead.
Form into balls and roll in confectioners sugar.

CHOCOLATE CHIP CANDY

1.   1 Package (18 oz.) Chocolate Chips
2.   1 Cup Chopped Nuts
3.   1 1/2 Teaspoon Vanilla
4.   1 Can (14 oz.) Sweetened Condensed Milk

Melt chips over low heat with sweetened condensed milk.
Remove from heat and stir in nuts and vanilla. Spread onto
wax paper lined 8x8-inch pan. Chill 2 hours. or until firm.
Cut into squares.

GOOD CANDY

1.   1 Package (12 oz.) Chocolate Chips
2.   1 Package (12 oz.) Butterscotch Chips
3.   2 Tablespoons Peanut Butter
4.   2 Cups Chopped Pecans

Melt chips in double boiler. Add peanut butter. Stir. Add
pecans. Mix well. Drop by teaspoonful on waxed paper.
Cool.

PARTY MINTS

1.   1 Package (8 oz.) Cream Cheese (softened)
2.   2 Boxes (16 oz. each) Powdered Sugar
3.   1 Teaspoon Peppermint Flavoring
4.   Food Coloring (your choice)

Gradually add cream cheese to sugar. Add food coloring and peppermint. The mixture will be very stiff. Form into balls and place on waxed paper. Flatten each ball with bottom of a glass. Dust with sugar if desired.

PEANUT BUTTER CUPS

1.   1 Box (16 oz.) Powdered Sugar (Sifted)
2.   1 Quart Peanut Butter
3.   1 Pound Margarine
4.   1 Package (12 oz.) Milk Chocolate Chips

Cream margarine and peanut butter. Add sugar. Knead with fingers. Spread into a 9x13-inch pan. Melt chocolate chips in double boiler and pour over peanut butter mixture. Refrigerate until firm. Cut into squares.

TUMBLEWEEDS

1.   1 Package (12 oz.) Butterscotch Chips
2.   2 Tablespoons Peanut Butter
3.   1 Can (12 oz.) Peanuts
4.   1 Can (4 oz.) Shoestring Potatoes

Melt chips and peanut butter in double boiler. Combine peanuts and shoestring potatoes to butterscotch mixture. Drop by teaspoonful onto waxed paper. Cool.

INDEX

For Additional Copies...

Please send me...

____ copies of **The Four Ingredient Cookbooks** @ $19.95 each $_____
(contains the 3 original cookbooks - Vol. I, II, and III)

____ copies of **The Diabetic Four Ingredient Cookbook** @ $19.95 each $_____
(New - contains over 352 diabetic recipes)

Postage & handling @ $3.50 each $_____

Sub-Total $_____

Texas residents add 8.25% sales tax per book @ $1.93 each $_____

Canadian orders add additional $6.60 per book $_____

Total Enclosed $_____

❏ Check enclosed made payable to "Coffee and Cale"

Or charge to my

❏ VISA   ❏ MasterCard   ❏ Discover   *(Canada - credit card only)*

Card # _____ Exp. Date _____

Ship to:

Name_____

Address _____Apt.# _____

City _____ State _____ Zip _____

E-mail address _____

Phone _____
(Must have for Credit Card Orders)

Coffee & Cale
P.O. Box 2121 • Kerrville, TX 78029 • 1-800-757-0838
www.fouringredientcookbook.com • email:areglen@ktc.com
For Wholesale Information: • (830) 895-5528

Also Available

Our *original* individual cookbooks!

____ copies of Vol. 1 T*he Four Ingredient Cookbook* @ $12.90 each $_____

____ copies of Vol. II *More of the Four Ingredient Cookbook* @ $12.90 each $_____

____ copies of Vol. III *Low-Fat & Light Four Ingredient Cookbook* @ $12.90 each $_____

Special Savings!!!
Buy any 3 original cookbooks for only $23.50!! $_____
above prices include shipping & handling of $2.95 per book

       Texas residents add 8.25% sales tax $_____
       Canadian orders add additional $3.30 per book $_____
       Total enclosed $_____

❏ Check enclosed made payable to "Coffee and Cale"
Or charge to my
❏ VISA   ❏ MasterCard   ❏ Discover *(Canada -credit card only)*

Card# _____
Exp. Date _____
Ship to:
Name _____
Address _____ Apt.# _____
City _____ State _____ Zip _____
E-mail address _____
Phone _____
(Must have for Credit Card Orders)

Coffee & Cale
P.O. Box 2121 • Kerrville, TX 78029 • 1-800-757-0838
www.fouringredientcookbook.com • email:areglen@ktc.com
For Wholesale Information: • (830) 895-5528